P9-DMH-096

It's My State!

KENTUCKY

The Bluegrass State

Ann Graham Gaines, William McGeveran, and Gerry Boehme

Cavendish
Square

New York

Published in 2017 by Cavendish Square Publishing, LLC
243 5th Avenue, Suite 136, New York, NY 10016

Copyright © 2017 by Cavendish Square Publishing, LLC

Third Edition

No part of this publication may be reproduced, stored in a retrieval system, or transmitted in any form or by any means—
electronic, mechanical, photocopying, recording, or otherwise—without the prior permission of the copyright owner.
Request for permission should be addressed to Permissions, Cavendish Square Publishing, 243 5th Avenue, Suite 136,
New York, NY 10016. Tel (877) 980-4450; fax (877) 980-4454.

Website: cavendishsq.com

This publication represents the opinions and views of the author based on his or her personal experience, knowledge, and
research. The information in this book serves as a general guide only. The author and publisher have used their best efforts in
preparing this book and disclaim liability rising directly or indirectly from the use and application of this book.

CPSIA Compliance Information: Batch #CS16CSQ

All websites were available and accurate when this book was sent to press.

Library of Congress Cataloging-in-Publication Data

Names: Gaines, Ann. | McGeveran, William. | Boehme, Gerry.
Title: Kentucky / Ann Graham Gaines, William McGeveran, and Gerry Boehme.
Description: New York : Cavendish Square Publishing, 2017. | Series: It's my
state! | Includes bibliographical references and index. | Description
based on print version record and CIP data provided by publisher; resource
not viewed.
Identifiers: LCCN 2016000174 (print) | LCCN 2015051337 (ebook)
ISBN 9781627132008 (ebook) | ISBN 9781627131988 (library bound)
Subjects: LCSH: Kentucky--Juvenile literature.
Classification: LCC F451.3 (print) | LCC F451.3 .G352 2017 (ebook)
DDC 976.9—dc23
LC record available at http://lccn.loc.gov/2016000174

Editorial Director: David McNamara
Editor: Fletcher Doyle
Copy Editor: Nathan Heidelberger
Art Director: Jeffrey Talbot
Designer: Stephanie Flecha
Production Assistant: Karol Szymczuk
Photo Research: J8 Media

The photographs in this book are used by permission and through the courtesy of: Glow Images, Inc/Glow/Getty Images, cover; James Urbach/Superstock, 4; Nancy Bauer/Shutterstock.
com, 4; GAP/Superstock, 4; Chris Mattison/Alamy, 5; David Byron Keener/Shutterstock.com, 5; Adrian Sherratt/Alamy, 5; Melinda Fawver/Shutterstock.com, 6; Tom Till/Superstock, 8;
Westgraphix LLC, 10; James Kirkikis/Superstock, 12; Danita Delimont/Gallo Images/Getty Images, 13; treewoman8/File:Big South Fork Scenic Railway.jpg/Wikimedia Commons, 14;
jessicakirsh/Shutterstock.com, 14; Shadle/File:Natural Arch Kentucky.jpg/Wikimedia Commons, 14; AP Photo/National Park Service, Gary Berdeaux, 15; © David Davis Photoproductions/
Alamy Stock Photo, 15; Danita Delimont/Getty Images, 15; Daniel Dempster Photography/Alamy, 16; Robert Harding Picture Library Ltd/Alamy, 17; Pat & Chuck Blackley, 18; Minden
Pictures/Superstock, 20; Design Pics Inc./Alamy, 20; David Byron Keener/Shutterstock.com, 20; Funkystock/age fotostock/Superstock, 21; Daniel Dempster Photography/Alamy, 21; Mark
Cassino/Superstock, 21; Education Images/UIG via Getty Images, 22; Ivy Close Images/Alamy, 24; Jim Lane/Alamy, 25; Sarah Cates/Shutterstock.com, 26; North Wind Picture Archives/Alamy,
28; Everett Historical/Shutterstock.com, 29; © FocusEurope/Alamy Stock Photo, 30; North Wind Picture Archives/Alamy, 32; Science Faction/Superstock, 33; Walter Bibikow/Jon Arnold
Images/Superstock, 34; AP Photo/The Messenger-Inquirer, John Dunham, 35; AP Photo/Al Behrman, File, 35; James R. Martin/Shutterstock.com, 35; North Wind Picture Archives, 36; AP
Photo, 37; AP Photo, 38; Bettmann/Corbis, 39; AP Photo, 41; Jonathan Newton/The Washington Post via Getty Images, 44; Bob Krist/Corbis, 47; AP Photo/Richard Drew, 48; Featureflash/
Shutterstock.com, 48; Debby Wong/Shutterstock.com, 48; AP Photo/Tammie Arroyo, 49; Theo Wargo/WireImage/Getty Images, 49; AP Photo/Peter Kramer, 49; David Davis/age fotostock/
Superstock, 51; Pat Canova/Alamy, 53; Courtesy of GSCTC, 54; Clay Jackson/The Advocate-Messenger via AP, 54; Daniel Dempster Photography/Alamy, 55; age fotostock/Superstock, 55;
Nagel Photography/Shutterstock.com, 56; Andre Jenny/Alamy, 58; Richard Cummins/Superstock, 59; Nomad/Superstock, 60; Niday Picture Library/Alamy, 62; Tom Williams/CQ Roll Call/
Getty Images, 62; AP Photo, 62; Charles Bertram/Lexington Herald-Leader/MCT via Getty Images, 64; Stock Connection/Superstock, 66; Robert Llewellyn/Superstock, 67; Visions of America/
Superstock, 68; Transtock/Superstock, 68; Belinda Images/Superstock, 69; AP Photo/Al Behrman, 69; L.Trott/Shutterstock.com, 70; Science Faction/Superstock, 73; Christopher Santoro, 74;
Jillian Cain/Shutterstock.com, 75; Matt Wasson, Appalachian Voices. April 18th, 2010/Kentucky Side of Black, Mountain/Flickr.com, 75; Christopher Santoro, 76.

Printed in the United States of America

KENTUCKY

★ ★ ★ ★

CONTENTS

State Bird: Cardinal

The cardinal lives in Kentucky throughout the year and sings nearly all year round. Male cardinals have bright red feathers, while females usually have brown feathers. Both have a jet-black mask, pronounced crest, and heavy bill. Cardinals eat seeds, small wild fruits, and insects.

State Fossil: Brachiopod

Brachiopods are the fossilized shells of creatures that once lived in the oceans and seas. Although they resemble clams, brachiopods are a different group of animal. Most are now extinct. The region that became Kentucky used to be underwater, and many different types of brachiopods are embedded in the rocks.

State Flower: Goldenrod

The spiky, yellow blossoms of goldenrod can be found in many parts of Kentucky. Bison, commonly called buffalo, roamed freely in the region long ago, and they helped spread goldenrod across wide areas. The goldenrod seeds would stick to the animals' fur and fall off as the herds traveled.

KENTUCKY

⭐ State Horse: **Thoroughbred**

Kentucky is well known for its horse farms and **Thoroughbred** horses. These horses, which are raised mostly for racing, feed on the state's bluegrass fields. Adult Thoroughbreds can weigh more than 1,000 pounds (450 kilograms), and they measure about 5 feet (1.5 meters) from shoulder to ground.

⭐ State Wild Animal Game Species: **Gray Squirrel**

Gray squirrels are common in American woodlands, parks, and backyards. The eastern gray squirrel usually has a range of 5 acres (2 hectares) or less. Although some eastern gray squirrels survive more than ten years in the wild, most live an average of only about one year.

⭐ State Tree: **Tulip Poplar**

The tulip, or yellow, poplar tree has beautiful yellow-green flowers that bloom in the spring. Native Americans and settlers used its wood to build canoes, homes, and furniture. Tulip poplars can live for more than one hundred years and grow to be more than 100 feet (30 m) tall.

The Big South Fork National River and
Recreation Area is a great place to view
the beauty of the landscape of Kentucky.

The Bluegrass State

When Stephen Foster wrote the lyrics to "My Old Kentucky Home, Good-Night!" in 1853, he was said to have been inspired by Federal Hill, the name of his cousins' home in Bardstown. He wrote:

> The sun shines bright in My Old Kentucky Home,
> 'Tis summer, the people are gay;
> The corn-top's ripe and the meadow's in the bloom
> While the birds make music all the day.

In truth, the lyrics describe the fabulous landscape across the entire state, filled with rich farmland, lush meadows, majestic mountains and picturesque cities. Kentucky's legislators obviously agreed, making "My Old Kentucky Home" the official state song back in 1928. Those words paint as true a picture of Kentucky today as they did when the song was written more than 160 years ago.

Kentucky is located in the east-central portion of the United States, on the upper fringe of the South. It is part of the so-called Upper South, as opposed to the Deep South, which

A natural pass through the Appalachian Mountains, called the Cumberland Gap, opened Kentucky for settlers.

includes states located in the lower, southern half of the US. Kentucky also borders the Midwest, and parts of the state are similar to that region.

Kentucky Borders

North:	Illinois
	Indiana
	Ohio
South:	Tennessee
East:	West Virginia
	Virginia
West:	Missouri
	Illinois
	Indiana

Kentucky's position between Northern and Southern states has played a role in its history. During the Civil War (1861–1865), Kentucky never withdrew, or seceded, from the Union, as did other Southern states. It remained a slave state, however, and many Kentuckians sided with the South in that bitter conflict.

It takes approximately six hours to drive across Kentucky. Even so, Kentucky is not a large state compared to many others in the country. It has a land area of only 39,486 square miles (102,269 square kilometers), which means that thirty-six states are bigger in land area than Kentucky. Despite its relatively small size, Kentucky is divided into

Let's Take A Cruise

Kentucky has more miles/kilometers of running water than any other state except Alaska. Ships and boats can travel more than 1,100 miles [1,770 km] in the state.

many counties—120 in all. Jefferson County, in the north, has the biggest population and is the most densely populated. Its county seat is Louisville, the state's biggest city.

Kentucky has an unusual shape. Its southern border is mostly straight, except for an interesting **jut** in the far west, where it extends down a bit toward Tennessee, its southern neighbor. However, the Ohio River provides Kentucky with a bumpy shape as it winds along the long northwestern and northern border, alongside Missouri, Ohio, Illinois, and Indiana. The state's eastern border comes to a sharp point that resembles the mouth of a fish as it bites into Virginia and West Virginia.

Regions of Kentucky

Kentucky can be divided into many different geographical regions. The Appalachian Mountains, which stretch from Canada to Alabama, cut through eastern Kentucky. This region, called the Appalachian, or Cumberland, Plateau, takes up about one-fourth of the state's land area. Black Mountain, the state's highest point, is located here. It stands 4,145 feet (1,263 m) above sea level. The Cumberland Gap, in the southeast, slices a path through the Appalachians along the borders of Kentucky, Tennessee, and Virginia. Cumberland Gap National Historic Park contains mountains covered in forests, with deep valleys, gorges, rivers, and streams. Large coal deposits can be found underground in this region of the state.

Stretching through part of eastern Kentucky is the Daniel Boone National Forest. This forest, managed and protected by the US Forest Service, includes more than 700,000 acres (280,000 ha) of land. Filled with cliffs, lakes, and streams, it is a popular attraction for lovers of the outdoors.

Cities, Farms, and Horses

The north-central portion of the state, known as the Bluegrass region, displays rolling hills and valleys. The Kentucky River flows through this area, and a large portion of the state's population lives there. The state's two biggest cities, Louisville and Lexington, are located here, as is Frankfort, the state capital. Interestingly, this area is also a center of agriculture and is well known as the center for one of Kentucky's most famous industries: raising horses.

Adair	18,656	Bullitt	74,319	Cumberland	6,856
Allen	19,956	Butler	12,690	Daviess	96,656
Anderson	21,421	Caldwell	12,984	Edmonson	12,161
Ballard	8,249	Calloway	37,191	Elliott	7,852
Barren	42,173	Campbell	90,336	Estill	14,672
Bath	11,591	Carlisle	5,104	Fayette	295,803
Bell	28,691	Carroll	10,811	Fleming	14,348
Boone	118,811	Carter	27,720	Floyd	39,451
Bourbon	19,985	Casey	15,955	Franklin	49,285
Boyd	49,542	Christian	73,955	Fulton	6,813
Boyle	28,432	Clark	35,613	Gallatin	8,589
Bracken	8,488	Clay	21,730	Garrard	16,912
Breathitt	13,878	Clinton	10,272	Grant	24,662
Breckinridge	20,059	Crittenden	9,315	Graves	37,121

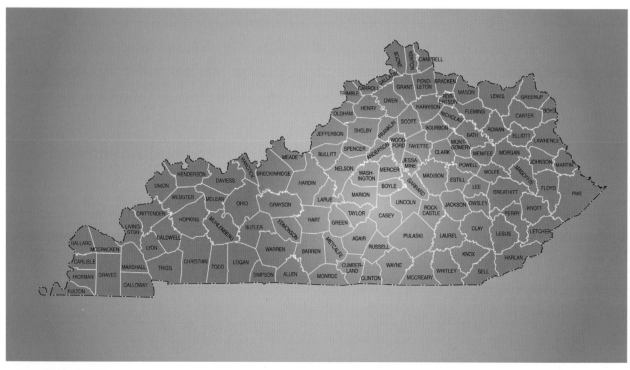

KENTUCKY

POPULATION BY COUNTY

County	Population	County	Population	County	Population
Grayson	25,746	Livingston	9,519	Perry	28,712
Green	11,258	Logan	26,835	Pike	65,024
Greenup	36,910	Lyon	8,314	Powell	12,613
Hancock	8,565	McCracken	65,565	Pulaski	63,063
Hardin	105,543	McCreary	18,306	Robertson	2,282
Harlan	29,278	McLean	9,531	Rockcastle	17,056
Harrison	18,846	Madison	82,916	Rowan	23,333
Hart	18,199	Magoffin	13,333	Russell	17,565
Henderson	46,250	Marion	19,820	Scott	47,173
Henry	15,416	Marshall	31,448	Shelby	42,074
Hickman	4,902	Martin	12,929	Simpson	17,327
Hopkins	46,920	Mason	17,490	Spencer	17,061
Jackson	13,494	Meade	28,602	Taylor	24,512
Jefferson	741,096	Menifee	6,306	Todd	12,460
Jessamine	48,586	Mercer	21,331	Trigg	14,339
Johnson	23,356	Metcalfe	10,099	Trimble	8,809
Kenton	159,720	Monroe	10,963	Union	15,007
Knott	16,346	Montgomery	26,499	Warren	113,792
Knox	31,883	Morgan	13,923	Washington	11,717
Larue	14,193	Muhlenberg	31,499	Wayne	20,813
Laurel	58,849	Nelson	43,437	Webster	13,621
Lawrence	15,860	Nicholas	7,135	Whitley	35,637
Lee	7,887	Ohio	23,842	Wolfe	7,355
Leslie	11,310	Oldham	60,316	Woodford	24,939
Letcher	24,519	Owen	10,841		
Lewis	13,870	Owsley	4,755		
Lincoln	24,742	Pendleton	14,877		

Source: US Bureau of the Census, 2010

Horse farms thrive in north-central Kentucky, which is known as the Bluegrass region.

Farmers in the Bluegrass region grow tobacco and corn, among other crops. The fertile soil also provides grass that horses can feed on. Horse farms breed horses that compete each year in the famous Kentucky Derby, perhaps the most famous horse race in the world.

To the east, south, and west of the Bluegrass region is a narrow belt of land. It is called the Knobs region because of its dome-shaped hills. To the south of that is an area of hills and rolling land that also extends westward along the state's southern border. Called the Pennyroyal Plateau, this region has no rivers because water from rainfall quickly seeps into the limestone rock below.

The Pennyroyal Plateau has many caves. These caves were carved out of limestone, which comes from the shells of ancient sea creatures that lived in that area many years ago when the land was covered by shallow water. Mammoth Cave National Park, in south-central Kentucky, contains the world's longest network of caves. The cave system formed over millions of years, as water seeped down through the ground and wore away parts of the limestone beneath. Passageways cover more than 350 miles (550 kilometers) in all. They extend almost 400 feet (120 m) below Earth's surface. Explorers of these caves continue to discover and map new passages.

The Frozen Niagara formation is one of many interesting features in Mammoth Cave National Park.

Rivers and streams run through the caves. Eyeless fish, cave shrimp, and cave crayfish swim in the dark waters. Bats have lived here for millions of years, though their numbers have sharply decreased over the years. Today, crickets are more common. Some two hundred types, or species, of animals have adapted to cave life, at least part time. They tend to be small and live for a very long period of time.

Artifacts such as tools and mummified remains of humans and animals have been found in Mammoth Cave, indicating that early Native Americans used the cave system. Later, settlers who came to the area from early colonies and from Europe also used and explored the caves. During the 1800s, the caves were mined for products such as saltpeter, an ingredient used to make gunpowder. The US government declared the area a national park in 1941. Mammoth Cave National Park is recognized as an official World Heritage Site because of its amazing natural features and historical importance.

North and west of the Pennyroyal Plateau, western Kentucky has rolling fields with fertile soil that is ideal for farming. The plains and hills stretch westward past the Mississippi and Ohio Rivers and beyond the state's borders. The region also has some swamps. Parts of western Kentucky, around the Green River and south of the Ohio River, have large coal deposits.

Land Formed by a Bend in the River

One small piece of Kentucky land—in the southwestern corner—is cut off from the rest of the state by the Mississippi River. Known by several names including the "Kentucky Bend" and "Bubbleland," this small area was once known for its rich soil, perfect for growing cotton. Today it consists mainly of some houses, a few farms, and some small fishing

★10★KEY SITES★ ★ ★

Big South Fork Scenic Railway

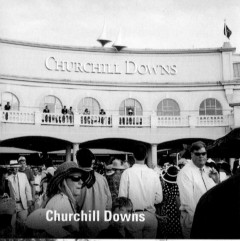

Churchill Downs

Daniel Boone National Forest

1. Big South Fork Scenic Railway

Travel to Stearns and take a 16-mile (26 km) trip on this historical railway into Daniel Boone National Forest. See spectacular scenery as you descend 600 feet (183 m) into a gorge before stopping at Blue Heron, an old coal mining camp.

2. Churchill Downs

One of the most famous locations in US sports, Louisville's Churchill Downs hosts the Kentucky Derby and many other horse races. It also includes a museum and features Family Fun Days, which offer games and crafts hosted by Churchill Charlie.

3. Cumberland Falls State Resort Park

Called "Niagara of the South," this state park is located near Corbin. It includes camping grounds and a museum, but its greatest attraction is the falls, stretching 65 feet tall (20 m) and 125 feet (38 m) wide.

4. Cumberland Gap National Historic Park

Located near Middlesboro, the Cumberland Gap has been called the "first great gateway to the west." It provided a path for bison, Native Americans, and pioneers to pass through the mountains into Kentucky.

5. Daniel Boone National Forest

Located southeast of Lexington, the Daniel Boone National Forest features rock formations and sandstone cliffs. The Natural Bridge (*left*), created by the forces of wind and water, measures 65 feet (20 m) high and 75 feet (23 m) wide.

KENTUCKY ★ ★ ★ ★

6. Great American Dollhouse Museum

Danville's Great American Dollhouse Museum showcases more than two hundred dollhouses, miniature buildings, and room boxes, furnished in remarkable detail and populated with tiny people at work and play. The museum uses miniature figures to depict times in American history.

7. Mammoth Cave National Park

The state's top attraction gets four hundred thousand visitors a year. About 10 miles (16 km) of passages in Mammoth Cave are open for guided tours, which can take six hours.

8. National Corvette Museum

Bowling Green's National Corvette Museum honors "America's Sports Car" by displaying more than eighty Corvettes, including mint classics, unique prototypes, and the newest editions. The museum sits less than 1 mile (1.6 km) from the assembly plant that produces all Corvettes today.

9. Newport Aquarium

Rated as one of the top aquariums in the country, Newport Aquarium hosts penguins, alligators, poisonous predators, and jellyfish. The rope suspension Shark Bridge provides guests with the thrill of walking just inches above nearly two dozen sharks.

10. Shaker Village of Pleasant Hill

Experience Kentucky's rich history and heritage at the Shaker Village in Harrodsburg. Explore the Living History Museum to meet the men and women who have called the village their home for more than one hundred years.

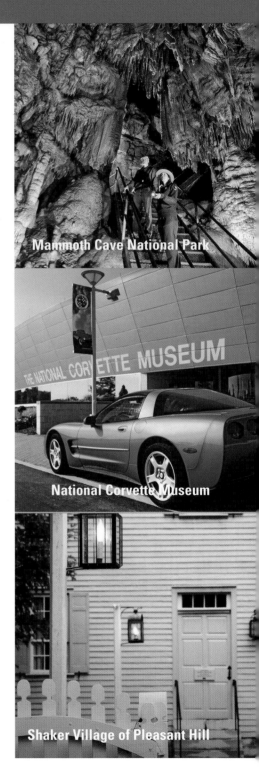

Mammoth Cave National Park

National Corvette Museum

Shaker Village of Pleasant Hill

The Ohio River forms a long part of Kentucky's border. Here it separates the state from Indiana.

lakes. You can only reach this area by road from Tennessee. Kids living on the Bend attend school in Tiptonville, Tennessee, which also provides the closest medical care and food stores. To vote in Kentucky elections, Benders must travel to the nearest voting machines in Hickman, Kentucky, which means a 40-mile (64 km) drive into Tennessee and then back into Kentucky.

Rivers and Lakes

Many rivers flow through Kentucky. The Mississippi and Ohio are two major rivers that run along the state's borders. Other rivers wind across Kentucky and empty into the Ohio. Large boats travel on the major rivers, carrying cargo between ports. The smaller rivers and streams often run through rocky gorges. Fish swim in these waters and wildlife lives along the shores.

Over the years, Kentuckians have built dams on some rivers in order to control the flow of water. The water is used to power huge turbines and produce hydroelectricity. These dams created artificial lakes. In the southwestern part of the state is Kentucky Lake, an artificial body of water more than 180 miles (290 km) long, created by a dam on the Tennessee River near the Ohio. To the east of Kentucky Lake is Lake Barkley, which was created by a dam on the Cumberland River. Lake Barkley is 118 miles (190 km) long, and for much of this length, it runs parallel to Kentucky Lake. The two lakes, joined together by a canal, make up the largest body of water between the Great Lakes and the Gulf of Mexico. Sitting in between the lakes is a big national recreation area called, sensibly enough, Land Between the Lakes, where people swim, boat, and fish.

There are only two very large waterfalls in the United States located east of the Rocky Mountains. One is Niagara Falls, in the Northeast, along the border between New York and Canada. The other is Cumberland Falls, in eastern Kentucky. Cumberland Falls is special not only for its size and beauty, but also because of what local residents call a "moonbow"—a silver arc reflecting the light of the moon—which can appear overhead on clear nights.

Climate

Kentucky has a temperate climate with warm summers and cool winters. In the summertime, temperatures usually range from around 70 to 80 degrees Fahrenheit (around 21 to 27 degrees Celsius). The average July temperature in Louisville from 1981 to 2010 was 79°F (26°C). The average winter temperature in Louisville from 1981 to 2010 was 35°F (2°C).

The weather in Kentucky is usually mild, but it can vary greatly. The state's highest temperature of 114°F (46°C) was recorded on July 28, 1930, in Greensburg. On the other

Cumberland Falls drops about 68 feet (21 m) at a spot where the Cumberland River is 125 feet (38 m) wide.

Mill Creek Lake provides a placid place for fishing.

hand, winters can get very cold. On January 19, 1994, the temperature in Shelbyville hit a record low for the state: −37°F (−38°C).

Kentucky gets a great deal of rain during the year, especially in the springtime. Snow also falls in the winter, but the average amount of snowfall can vary greatly by region. In the northern part of the state, the mountains get enough snow for skiing during the cold months.

Wildlife

For centuries, many different species of animals roamed the land freely, including herds of elk and bison, as well as bears, wolves, and cougars. Hunting and the loss of natural habitat decreased or virtually eliminated some animal populations over the years. Although bison no longer live on the land, elk continue to be found, bears have returned, and coyotes have arrived from the north and southwest, taking the place of wolves. Deer roam the woods and fields throughout the state.

Many of Kentucky's mammals are smaller animals such as raccoons, foxes, rabbits, squirrels, and opossums. River otters live along rivers and streams. Nature enthusiasts— as well as people who like to fish—can find catfish, bass, bluegill, perch, and trout in Kentucky's waters. Kentucky's wilds are also home to many species of snakes, including rattlesnakes, copperheads, and water moccasins. There are also frogs, turtles, and lizards.

More than three hundred species of birds live in Kentucky or fly each year through the western part of the state, which is a major migration route. There are birds of prey, such as bald eagles, hawks, and owls, as well as pheasants, ducks, geese, and smaller birds such as blue jays, cardinals, wrens, and chickadees.

Kentucky is home to more than two thousand species of plants. In the springtime, wildflowers bloom across meadows, forests, and mountainsides, and even along highways. Plants such as jack-in-the-pulpit, goldenrod, Cumberland sandwort, and rosemary thrive in Kentucky's fertile soil. Mountain laurels, azaleas, rhododendrons, bluebells, violets, and bloodroot can also be found throughout the state. Huge trees such as cypress grow along the rivers, while water plants spring up in the shallow waters.

In all, hundreds of different types of trees grow in the state's forests, including elm, ash, hickory, maple, oak, willow, poplar, cedar, hemlock, and pine. Many of these forests are second growth. This means they are made up of new trees planted after older and larger trees were cut down.

Protecting Nature

About fifty species of plants and animals in Kentucky are considered endangered (in danger of dying out completely) or threatened (close to being endangered). These include eight fish species, at least twenty species of mussels, and four species of bats: the Indiana bat, gray bat, Northern long-eared bat, and Virginia big-eared bat. Bat Conservation International and other groups, together with government agencies, work to preserve and restore caves, abandoned mines, and other bat-friendly places. These groups also organize to fight white nose syndrome, a deadly bat disease, and to educate the public about the **ecological** importance of bats.

Over the years, Kentucky's wilderness has shrunk in size. Forests were cleared to create fields and pastures and to make room for highways, towns, and cities. As the lumber industry grew, trees were cut down in large numbers and sent down the rivers to be sold. Clear-cutting the forests has left mountaintops and hillsides bare.

Some of these areas have been restored, however, and 40 to 50 percent of the land in Kentucky today is wooded. Kentuckians are very aware of the need to preserve this natural wilderness. While state parks and nature preserves protect a small part of Kentucky's land, the state government also supports efforts to conserve wildlife on privately owned **plots** of all sizes. For example, the Kentucky Department of Fish and Wildlife Resources has a program called Backyard Wildlife that helps Kentuckians set up bird feeders and plant flowers to attract butterflies.

Black Bear

Bluegrass

Five-Lined Skink

1. Black Bear

Black bears swim, climb trees, and can run quickly over short distances. They feed on plants, insects, fish, and animals. Black bears almost disappeared in Kentucky as wooded areas were lost to logging, but they have been returning in the past twenty years.

2. Bluegrass

The grass that gave Kentucky its nickname, bluegrass, is actually green, but in the spring its bluish-purple buds give large fields a blue appearance. Bluegrass was imported into Kentucky from Europe in the early colonial days.

3. Copperhead

Kentucky's most common **venomous** snake, copperheads grow to be about 2 feet (61 cm) long. They feature dark hourglass crossbands on a lighter brown to rust background. Copperheads eat rodents, lizards, large caterpillars, and cicadas. Their bite is rarely fatal.

4. Coyote

Coyotes roam throughout Kentucky, including suburban areas, where people can hear them howling at night. They have strong senses of smell, sight, and hearing and can weigh up to 50 pounds (23 kg). Coyotes eat grass, insects, mice, rabbits, and even livestock.

5. Five-Lined Skink

The five-lined skink is an insect-eating lizard that can grow up to 8 inches (20.3 cm) long. They are usually black or dark brown, with five light stripes down their backs.

KENTUCKY ★ ★ ★ ★

6. Kentucky Bass

The Kentucky (or spotted) bass is usually about 12 inches (30 cm) long and may weigh up to 10 pounds (4.5 kg). This freshwater fish can live as long as seven years and is known for its fighting ability.

7. Paddlefish

The paddlefish (also called spoonfish) is a large, shark-like fish with a paddle-shaped snout. The largest freshwater fish in the United States, paddlefish can grow to be more than 200 pounds (91 kg) and 6 feet (1.8 m) long. They are prized for their white meat.

8. Saint John's Wort

This plant grows in the fields and forests in many parts of Kentucky. The plant can reach more than 1 foot (30 cm) in height and has yellow flowers. Saint John's wort is used in herbal medicines.

9. White-Tailed Deer

White-tailed deer live in forests, on farmlands, and even around suburban areas of Kentucky. Their color varies from light brown to gray, but the underside of their tail is white. White spots help fawns blend in with their surroundings.

10. Viceroy Butterfly

Kentucky's state butterfly, the viceroy, resembles the larger monarch butterfly. While the monarch is poisonous to predators, the viceroy butterfly is not. However, birds still won't eat the viceroy because it looks so much like the monarch.

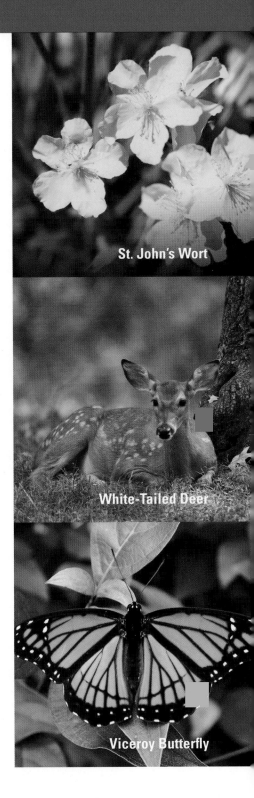

St. John's Wort

White-Tailed Deer

Viceroy Butterfly

The Gladie Cabin was built in the late 1800s. It is located in the Red River Gorge.

From the Beginning

Historians believe that Kentucky's name is based on a Native American word, though no one knows for sure what language it comes from or what the word's exact meaning was. It might have been passed down from a word that meant "meadow land" or "land of tomorrow."

Before humans lived in what is now Kentucky, herds of mammoths (large animals that resembled furry elephants), musk oxen, and bison roamed the land. At least twelve thousand years ago, humans came to the area. They may have been hunters following herds of mammoths or bison. These earliest Kentuckians were descendants of Asian people who had arrived on the West Coast of the Americas many centuries before, probably crossing a land bridge that once connected Asia to Alaska. Archaeologists, who study the remains of cultures from the distant past, think these first Kentucky people hunted in small groups with spears and built temporary shelters. Scientists believe the climate was cold and wet compared to today.

By about 8000 BCE, scientists believe the climate had warmed, and the biggest animals had died out. The region's early Native Americans fished, hunted smaller animals, collected wild plants, and lived in seasonal camps. Eventually these people learned to grow vegetables such as squash.

During the so-called Woodland Period, around 1000 BCE to 1000 CE, Native Americans learned to make pottery, which they used to store food. They grew and harvested corn and tobacco, traded goods over long distances, and eventually developed the bow and arrow. After about 1000 CE, Native Americans relied more heavily on crops such as corn and beans. They lived year-round in communities of perhaps as many as two thousand residents, ruled by chiefs.

Groups of Native people who once lived in the western part of what is now Kentucky built large mounds from dirt and clay. These were used as places of religious worship and as tombs. Inside the mounds, archaeologists have found skeletal remains, along with tools, pottery, and other valuables.

By the time European explorers came to the Kentucky area, large native settlements had disappeared and few Native Americans still lived in the region. Tribes who lived mostly elsewhere, including the Iroquois, the Shawnee, the Cherokee, and the Chickasaw, came to the Kentucky region to hunt. As Europeans began to explore and settle the area, the Native Americans who visited or lived in the region died in large numbers because they lacked immunity to diseases that the Europeans brought with them.

Europeans Arrive

In the early 1670s, two Frenchmen—Louis Jolliet, an explorer, and Jacques Marquette, a Jesuit missionary priest—traveled down the Mississippi River. On the way, they passed through today's western Kentucky, where they met groups of Native Americans. Though records of the time are not clear, these Native Americans were probably members of the Shawnee tribe. In 1674, an

Father Louis Hennepin explored parts of the Mississippi River in the late 1600s, often traveling by canoe.

English explorer named Gabriel Arthur entered what is now Kentucky from the east. For a long time, no other traders and explorers tried to reach the area from the east, since the Appalachian Mountains were very hard to cross. However, exploration from the west continued.

In 1679, the French explorer René-Robert Cavelier, sieur de La Salle (now commonly referred to as La Salle), began exploring the Mississippi region, accompanied for a time by a Dutch priest named Louis Hennepin. Eventually, La Salle traveled down the length of the Mississippi by canoe. It is believed that during their expedition, La Salle and his men met Native Americans of the Iroquois tribes in what is now western Kentucky. La Salle and his men eventually reached the mouth of the Mississippi, where it empties into the Gulf of Mexico, and La Salle claimed all the lands along the river for France.

During the 1700s, both France and Great Britain wanted to control the Ohio River and its surrounding territory. People living to the east in Virginia—which was a British colony—ignored French claims to the Ohio River area. Instead, Virginia's government encouraged its people to form organizations called land companies to help settlers move west beyond the Appalachians. Control over this land would make Virginia bigger and more powerful.

This idealized painting shows Daniel Boone and his followers blazing the Wilderness Road through the Cumberland Gap into Kentucky.

The Native People

Native Americans lived in the area we now call Kentucky thousands of years before Kentucky pioneers arrived. The ancestors of these earliest Kentuckians may have come to the Western Hemisphere as early as 16,500 years ago by crossing a strip of land, now submerged beneath the Bering Strait, which connected the Asian and North American continents. These first peoples lived as nomads, constantly moving to follow and hunt large game animals. They built permanent settlements as they developed more reliable food supplies, including small game, fish, roots, plants, and berries. These earliest inhabitants left hundreds of mounds and other structures scattered across the landscape.

When European explorers and settlers began entering Kentucky in the mid-1700s, there were few permanent Native American settlements in the region. Due to the abundance of wild game, the country was used as common hunting grounds by Shawnees from the north and Cherokees and Chickasaws from the south. While these and other tribes such as the Iroquois often claimed possession of the lands, no tribe was strong enough to occupy and permanently hold the area.

Though most of Kentucky's Native Americans did not settle the area themselves, they became increasingly hostile to the new European settlers who were moving in and taking over their hunting grounds. Many bloody conflicts followed, and some Native American tribes sided with the British during the Revolutionary War. When the colonists defeated Great Britain in the war and gained their independence, Native Americans lost most of their power in the area. They continued to raid settlements for a time, but Native American resistance to settlers largely ended by around 1814.

Unlike many other states, no federally recognized Native American tribes live in Kentucky today. The federal government forced many tribes to leave the state in the 1800s, relocating them

A Trail of Tears powwow is held every year in Hopkinsville.

to Oklahoma and other western states and territories. Those that remained often faced hardship and discrimination from the whites who settled the area, so they sometimes hid their Native American heritage. Descendants of the Cherokee and other tribes still live in Kentucky, but most people from those and other tribes live in other states.

Spotlight on the Cherokee

The Cherokee lived in the southeastern US, including Kentucky, Georgia, North and South Carolina, Virginia, and Tennessee. Most Cherokee were forced to march in the 1830s along the **Trail of Tears** to Oklahoma, where many of their descendants live today.

Homes: The Cherokee lived in villages, usually located near a river. Houses were made of river cane and plaster, with thatched roofs. These dwellings were about as strong and warm as log cabins.

Government: Cherokee bands were led by one war chief and one peace chief. Cherokee chiefs were chosen by a tribal **council**. Cherokee war chiefs were male, but the peace chief could be female.

Clothing: Cherokee men wore breechcloths and leggings. They usually shaved their heads except for a single scalplock. Cherokee women always wore their hair long and wore wraparound skirts and poncho-style blouses made out of woven fiber or deerskin. Both wore moccasins on their feet.

Language: Cherokee is pronounced "CHAIR-uh-kee," which means "speakers of another language." Most Cherokee people speak English today, but some also speak the Cherokee language, which is complex and has many soft sounds. Examples of Cherokee words include *osiyo* (pronounced oh-see-yoh), a friendly greeting, and *wado* (pronounced wah-doh), which means "thank you."

Food: The Cherokee grew crops like corn, beans, and squash and gathered berries, nuts, and fruit. They also hunted small game and fished in the rivers. Cherokee foods included cornbread, soups, and stews cooked on stone hearths.

Crafts: Traditional Cherokee art included pipe carving, rivercane baskets, and pottery.

In 1750, Thomas Walker, a doctor from Virginia, found a passage through a low point in the Appalachian Mountains. Though Native Americans had used this route for centuries, it was not familiar to the colonists. This path came to be known as the Cumberland Gap. One year later, another explorer, Christopher Gist, crossed the Kentucky region.

Settlers did not quickly follow these adventurers, however. Most people were not yet ready to leave their homes in Virginia for the uncharted wilderness beyond the Appalachians. Exploration was also slowed by the French and Indian War (1754–1763). This war pitted France against Great Britain, with different Native American tribes joining each side. Great Britain eventually won the war and gained the lands west of the Appalachian Mountains and east of the Mississippi River, including what is now Kentucky.

Daniel Boone, a famous hunter and explorer, traveled to Kentucky in 1769, taking his first of many trips to the region. A few years later, in 1774, a group of colonists founded Harrodsburg. This settlement—the first permanent white settlement in Kentucky—was named after James Harrod, the leader of the group. In the beginning, the settlement was only a fort surrounded by a few cabins, but it expanded.

In 1775, Daniel Boone used the Cumberland Gap to lead settlers into Kentucky. The trail that he blazed—or established—was called the Wilderness Road. It ended at the Ohio River, where the city of Louisville stands today. Boone established Fort Boonesborough along the Kentucky River, and many colonists followed his Wilderness Road, settling in different parts of Kentucky.

The Wilderness Road allowed many settlers to reach Kentucky and quickly increase its population.

From Colony to State

The American Revolution began in 1775. During the war, Native Americans who sided with the British attacked colonial settlements in the Kentucky region. Settlers led by Boone and other Kentuckians successfully defended their land without outside help, but many lost their lives.

The war ended in 1783 with the Treaty of Paris, in which Great Britain recognized American independence. During that time, Kentucky was still legally part of Virginia. Since mountains cut it off from the rest of Virginia, it had to function mostly on its own. Many residents believed that Kentucky should be separated from Virginia, and the Virginia legislature agreed.

A Commonwealth

Kentucky's first constitution was drafted in April 1792. On June 1, 1792, Kentucky officially became a separate US state, choosing Isaac Shelby as its first governor. It was the first new state to be formed west of the Appalachian Mountains. When Kentucky became a state, it also chose to be known as a "commonwealth."

During the American Revolution, the colonies of Massachusetts, Virginia, and Pennsylvania declared themselves commonwealths. The word commonwealth was used at that time to show that the government existed for the common "weal," or welfare, of

The skill of the Kentucky riflemen helped Andrew Jackson defeat the British at the Battle of New Orleans.

Making a Racing Horse on a Stick

Kentucky is known for its horses. There are more than 320,000 horses in Kentucky and about 450 Thoroughbred horse farms in the state. Nearly 195,000 Kentuckians are involved in the industry as horse owners, service providers, employees, and volunteers. Even more participate as spectators. Each year, Louisville hosts the Kentucky Derby, the most famous horse race in the world.

Many Kentucky children like to make their own racehorses, using a stick for the body and a stuffed sock as its head. You can make your own racing horse in the same way.

What You Need

Broom with wooden handle (or a similar wooden stick)	Yarn
	Ribbons
One thick sock	Rope or string
Cotton material to use for stuffing	A needle
Two big buttons	Felt

What To Do

- Unscrew the broom from the handle.
- Fill the sock with stuffing. Stuff the sock as full as possible but leave the end of the sock under-stuffed. This will be the horse's head.
- Sew the buttons on each side of the sock. These will be the horse's eyes.
- Sew the felt on for nostrils, ears, and mouth.
- Use the yarn to make a mane. Sew the yarn onto the back of the horse's head, then cut it to a good length.
- Add ribbons as reins so you can hold on to the horse.
- Stick the wooden broom handle into the tube of the sock. Tie the sock onto the handle with string or rope.

its people and that the area was governed by the people instead of a monarch or king. Colonists wanted to make it clear that that they were independent and no longer ruled by the British.

When these former colonies became states, they decided to keep calling themselves commonwealths as well. At the time, Kentucky was part of Virginia. When Kentucky became its own state, Kentuckians also chose to keep the commonwealth name.

After Kentucky became a state, settlers began to arrive in very large numbers. In 1790, Kentucky only had about 74,000 people living there. By 1800, just ten years later, the new state had more than 220,000 people. Fifty years later, by 1860, there were more than one million Kentuckians.

Some seven thousand Kentuckians fought in the War of 1812 against Great Britain. In the Battle of New Orleans, Kentucky riflemen made up one-fourth of the army led by General Andrew Jackson, which won an overwhelming victory over the British. After the war, however, the country was in debt and prices rose sharply. During the economic crisis that followed, called the Panic of 1819, many Kentuckians suffered great hardships.

From Farms to Cities

During the early years of statehood, most Kentuckians made their living from the land. They grew and harvested crops such as corn, rye, tobacco, and hemp (which was used to make rope). Over time, Kentucky's towns and cities grew in population. Louisville, located on the Ohio River, became an important trade center and port. At first, rafts and flatboats (rectangular-shaped boats with flat bottoms) carried goods along the Ohio. Steamboats later made it possible to transport greater amounts of cargo and even more passengers.

Farmers brought their crops to Louisville, where they could be shipped down the Ohio and Mississippi Rivers, often all the way to New Orleans. From New Orleans, goods could be sent to states on the Atlantic coast or to countries in Central America, South America, or Europe.

The Civil War

The Civil War broke out in April 1861. Southern troops attacked Fort Sumter, a US Army post in the harbor of Charleston, South Carolina. Conflict between the South and the North had been brewing for years over the issue of slavery. The economy in the Deep South depended heavily on crops raised by slaves on large plantations. Slavery was very important to the economy in Kentucky, although in Kentucky more slaves worked on smaller farms than on plantations.

Some slaves in Kentucky worked on plantations, but most were owned by small farmers.

People in the North did not have the same need for slaves. Many Northerners believed that slavery was morally wrong, and it was abolished in most Northern states over the years. Northerners in particular did not want slavery extended to new areas of the country that were being settled. This issue led to a series of compromises between North and South in the US Congress. An influential senator from Kentucky named Henry Clay led the effort to reach these compromises.

When Abraham Lincoln was elected president in November 1860, many Southerners saw a threat to their way of life. Lincoln was personally opposed to slavery, and he had said that, as president, he would try to prevent its expansion into territories in the West.

By the time Lincoln took office as the sixteenth US president on March 4, 1861, seven states had decided to secede, or leave, the United States. They formed a breakaway nation called the Confederate States of America. After Fort Sumter fell to Confederate forces, Lincoln called for troops to fight against the Confederacy. Four more Southern states seceded.

The state of Kentucky did not secede from the US. Instead, Kentucky tried to remain neutral. However, people in the state were bitterly divided over the issue of slavery and whether to support the Confederate states. Southern supporters in Kentucky formed a rival Confederate government, in Bowling Green, but it lasted for only a short time.

A good example of how the issues of slavery and secession split Kentuckians is the fact that the leaders for both sides in the conflict were both born in Kentucky. Abraham Lincoln, sixteenth president of the United States, led the North, also called the Union, during the Civil War. On the other side, Jefferson Davis served as the first and only president of the Confederacy.

Abraham Lincoln was born in a one-room log cabin at Sinking Spring Farm, near the town of Hodgenville, in 1809. Although the cabin no longer exists, a replica has been built there to mark the spot. Jefferson Davis was born in Fairview in 1808. His birthplace is marked by a monument on a state historic site. Lincoln and Davis were born less than a year apart and fewer than 100 miles (161 km) away from each other.

Because of this division, men from Kentucky wound up fighting on both sides in the Civil War. More than seventy-five thousand Kentucky citizens fought for the North. More than thirty thousand joined the Confederate army. Due to its important location between Northern and Southern states, several important battles were fought on Kentucky soil. The biggest battle took place near Perryville in October 1862, when Confederate fighters were pitted against a stronger Union force. The

The election of Kentucky native Abraham Lincoln as president caused Southern states to secede from the Union.

Louisville

Owensboro

1. Louisville/Jefferson: population 597,337

Founded in 1778, Louisville was named in honor of King Louis XVI of France for helping the colonies during the Revolutionary War. Its location on the Ohio River made Louisville a major port. Louisville merged with Jefferson County in 2003.

2. Lexington-Fayette: population 295,803

Named after Lexington, Massachusetts, by early settlers when they heard that the first shots of the American Revolution had been fired there, Lexington today is known as the "Horse Capital of the World." Lexington merged with Fayette County in 1974.

3. Bowling Green: population 58,067

Founded in the late 1700s as a commercial and transportation center, Bowling Green is known for entertainment, manufacturing, and education. Chevrolet's Corvette "Stingray" sports car is built in the city and featured in a museum.

4. Owensboro: population 57,265

Owensboro is the industrial, medical, retail, and cultural hub of western Kentucky. Located on the southern banks of the Ohio River, Owensboro is full of charm, history, and Southern lifestyle. Festivals abound, offering unique visitor experiences.

5. Covington: population 40,640

Covington is located where the Ohio and Licking Rivers come together, immediately south of Cincinnati, Ohio. Covington's most popular destination for visitors, Mainstrasse Village, is a thriving entertainment and dining district.

KENTUCKY ★ ★ ★

6. Hopkinsville: population 31,577

Hopkinsville's agricultural roots date back to the 1790s. The area has been a leader in the production of corn, winter wheat, soybeans, and tobacco. Many companies are based there, including one of the largest makers of bowling balls.

7. Richmond: population 31,364

Richmond was founded in 1798 by Colonel John Miller, a Revolutionary War soldier. The site of a major Civil War battle in 1862, Richmond has recently experienced significant growth, rising from Kentucky's eleventh-largest city in 2000 to seventh in 2010.

8. Florence: population 29,951

Florence was originally known as Crossroads because of the **convergence** of several roads. It grew quickly after the completion of the Covington-Lexington Turnpike in 1836. Nearby interstate highways and an international airport give Florence a convenient location.

9. Georgetown: population 29,098

Founded at the site of a natural spring which still supplies it with water, Georgetown has expanded its economy from farming to include manufacturing and small business. Toyota built its first US assembly plant here in 1985.

10. Henderson: population 28,757

Henderson was once the country's richest community per person due to its production of tobacco. The city is home to John James Audubon State Park, Ellis Park Race Course, and a one-thousand-seat fine arts center.

Florence

TOYOTA MOTOR MANUFACTURI
VISITOR ENTRANCE

Georgetown

Union troops drove the Confederate army out of Kentucky with a victory in a battle near Perryville.

Confederates eventually withdrew and moved into Tennessee, leaving Union troops in control of Kentucky for the rest of the war.

After the War

In April 1865, the Civil War ended with the surrender of the South, and the Confederate states returned to the Union. While Kentucky never abolished slavery on its own, slavery was finally eliminated in the state when the Thirteenth Amendment to the US Constitution was approved later in the year. The Thirteenth Amendment outlawed slavery nationwide.

For a time, the economy of Kentucky suffered. Before the war, the state's farmers had sold many of their crops to other Southerners. After the war, most Southern states did not have much money to spend on Kentucky produce. Many farmers went bankrupt.

From the 1870s to the early 1900s, the state's economy started to improve. Tobacco continued to be an important crop, and coal mining in Kentucky became a major industry. Trains were fueled by coal, and as more railroads were built across America, demand for Kentucky coal increased. Logging also grew into a sizable business.

Changing Times

On April 6, 1917, the United States entered World War I (1914–1918) by declaring war on Germany. More than forty thousand Kentuckians fought overseas, and more than two thousand of them died.

After the war ended in 1918, times were hard for Kentucky's farmers and miners. Miners in particular had a difficult time. In Kentucky, as in other states rich in coal, many towns were founded near coal mines. The population grew as workers came to the state looking for jobs and the hope for a better life.

However, when these new workers arrived to work in the mines, they found that the coal companies were in total control. The companies managed the mines and owned all the equipment. Miners actually had to pay the mining companies to use their tools and live in the housing near the mines. The fees were very high and were often taken out of the miners' pay. Worst of all, the mines were unsafe and the work was extremely dangerous.

Labor Wars

Across many states, workers from factories, mills, mines, and other industries banded together in the 1880s to improve their lives. They wanted to fight the large controlling companies for better pay and safer working conditions. The groups that came together were called unions. The union created specifically for miners was called the United Mine Workers of America, or UMWA. Sometimes miners walked off the job, setting off a strike. A strike is when workers stop working in order to make one or more demands. Some of the things these miners wanted included the right to organize and get better pay, safer working conditions, and a nine-hour workday. Strikes often resulted in violent clashes between the miners and mining companies.

The Great Depression forced many people in Kentucky to live in horrible conditions.

The Great Depression

Strikes led to some improvement in miners' wages and working conditions. In 1929, however, conditions became much worse when the US **stock market** crashed. Banks failed across the United States, and many people lost their savings and

The first shipment of gold bars to Fort Knox arrived in January 1937. The building holds most of the gold reserves of the US government.

could not pay for their homes. Without money, people could not afford to buy goods, leading many companies that made those goods to collapse.

This great slowdown in economic activity eventually brought about the Great Depression. During this nationwide economic crisis that lasted through the 1930s, many coal miners lost their jobs, and farms failed across the state. Farmers and miners moved in large numbers to the cities in search of work.

The Great Depression touched almost everyone in the United States. To help provide relief for the suffering country, President Franklin D. Roosevelt created a set of programs that would help put people back to work and rebuild the country. These programs came to be known as the "New Deal."

Thousands of Kentuckians worked for New Deal programs such as the Civilian Conservation Corps and the Works Progress Administration. These programs provided income to many Kentucky families while also helping to build roads, parks, and other projects that Kentucky still uses today. Thousands of Kentuckians kept their homes through loans from another New Deal program called the Home Owners' Loan Corporation.

On the morning of December 7, 1941, Japan attacked the US Navy base at Pearl Harbor, Hawaii. The United States officially entered World War II (1939–1945) the next day. Brave Kentuckians fought for their country in both Europe against Germany and its allies and the Pacific against Japan. About eight thousand were killed or wounded.

During World War II, factories that produced war supplies were built across the state of Kentucky. The war resulted in a huge growth in industry that provided Kentuckians with much-needed jobs. Soon, farming was no longer the basis of Kentucky's economy.

Racial Discrimination

During the mid-1900s, race relations became more and more of a major issue for Kentuckians. For years, African-American Kentuckians had been legally **prohibited** from using the same restaurants, beaches, parks, restrooms, and other public facilities that white people used. Black schoolchildren had to attend separate, or "segregated," schools not attended by white children. These schools weren't as good as those for white children.

Black and white students enter a high school together as classrooms were finally integrated in Louisville in 1956.

Top Dog

A brass plate in the sidewalk at the corner of Limestone and Main Streets in downtown Lexington serves as a memorial marker honoring Smiley Pete. The animal, known as Lexington's town dog, died in 1957.

African Americans, joined by some white Kentuckians, protested these laws, and there were some changes in the 1940s and early 1950s. For example, in 1948, Louisville opened its public library to African Americans. Soon after that, African Americans were allowed to join the police force and fire department.

In 1954, the US Supreme Court ruled that having separate schools for blacks and whites violated the US Constitution. Many white people strongly resisted ending segregation in education, and for a time, many schools in Kentucky remained segregated. Eventually, state and local governments in Kentucky took some significant steps toward extending equal rights to African Americans. In 1963, the city council of Louisville passed a law against barring people from public facilities because of their race. Louisville was one of the first Southern cities to pass such a law. In 1966, the state legislature passed a major civil rights law that barred discrimination against African Americans in public facilities and jobs. It also gave cities the power to make laws to prevent discrimination in housing.

Poverty

Eastern Kentucky is part of a larger region of the southern Appalachian Mountains commonly known as Appalachia. Though this is an area of tremendous mineral wealth, its people have often been very poor. In the years after World War II, many miners and other workers in Appalachia lost their jobs.

During the mid-1960s, Appalachia gained national attention. Standing on a porch in an Appalachian town in Kentucky, President Lyndon B. Johnson announced legislation that he called his War on Poverty. Federal programs were created in Appalachia and throughout the country to improve living standards for America's poor. Included were the

"Oil's Well" in Kentucky

People may not think of Kentucky when they think of oil, but the first commercial oil well in the US was drilled in 1819 along the banks of the Cumberland River in McCreary County.

Medicaid and Medicare health insurance programs, food stamps for the hungry, and a program for the early education of low-income children called Head Start.

The coal mines of eastern Kentucky have long provided employment to the state's workers. This photo was taken in 1948.

Since the 1960s, conditions in Appalachia have improved, but even today, some of the poorest counties in the United States are in the Appalachian region of Kentucky. One of the problems in the area is that, as the coal business declined, no other source of income rose to take its place. The government has stepped in to try to help the people in the area and create new job programs, but the problem remains severe.

One of the reasons is that the area is remote, far from major highways. That makes it hard to ship goods and expensive to build a warehouse or a factory. People live in small communities located far apart, so many businesses don't want to move there. Many workers in the area also do not have the education or training that would help them compete in a modern business

In Their Own Words

"I hope to have God on my side, but I must have Kentucky."
—US president Abraham Lincoln

world. While some families can afford to move away to look for a better life in another area, other families are trapped.

Some parts of Kentucky have more economic resources than others, so people have raised concerns about the quality of education that children in poorer areas receive. Because local property taxes are the main source of funding for public schools, wealthier school districts have more money to spend.

No Deadly Duels Allowed

Even today, Kentucky governors must swear an oath before they take office that they have never fought a duel with deadly weapons.

In 1989, the Kentucky Supreme Court ruled that school districts, rich or poor, should have equal resources to fund their public schools. To meet this demand, the state legislature created a new system of state aid. The new system for funding schools can help provide a better education for all. The state of Kentucky has also adopted new educational standards and a testing program to help ensure these standards are met. Improved education can better provide students with the needed skills to succeed in today's economy.

Today's Challenges

Kentucky, like other states, was hit hard by the economic downturn, or recession, that began in late 2007. Between December 2007 and the middle of 2009, the state lost about 110,000 jobs. It took until 2014, seven years later, for Kentucky to climb back to the number of jobs it had in 2007.

Kentucky in the early twenty-first century faces serious problems, such as unemployment, poverty, and environmental concerns. Citizens have become more aware of the need to protect and preserve the environment. Industries such as tourism and automobile manufacturing have helped provide a boost to the economy. Kentuckians are working hard to deal with all the challenges they face, and they hope to create a bright and prosperous future for their state.

10 KEY DATES IN STATE HISTORY

1. ca. 1000 BCE-1000 CE

A mound-building Native American culture flourishes in areas that are now part of Kentucky.

2. April 17, 1750

Thomas Walker discovers a pathway through the Appalachian Mountains, later called the Cumberland Gap, while exploring land west of the Allegheny Mountains.

3. March 10, 1775

Daniel Boone leads a mission to explore territory along an old Native American trail. He carves a path, later called the "Wilderness Road."

4. June 1, 1792

Kentucky becomes the fifteenth state after splitting from Virginia, becoming the first state west of the Appalachian Mountains and one of four states to call itself a "commonwealth."

5. October 8, 1862

The Union army forces Confederate units to retreat into Tennessee at the Battle of Perryville, the largest and most costly Civil War battle in Kentucky.

6. January 13, 1937

Fort Knox becomes a major depository for government gold reserves when it receives its first shipment of gold bullion, worth $200 million.

7. January 27, 1966

Kentucky becomes the first Southern state to pass a civil rights act barring discrimination against African Americans in housing and employment.

8. November 8, 1983

Martha Layne Collins becomes Kentucky's first woman governor. When elected, she became the only female governor in the US at that time.

9. April 2, 2012

The University of Kentucky Wildcats win the National Collegiate Athletic Association (NCAA) Men's Division I Basketball Championship, their eighth national title.

10. February 12, 2014

A sinkhole causes the collapse of part of the National Corvette Museum in Bowling Green, damaging eight cars. Museum attendance increased as visitors come to see the hole.

Bluegrass has its roots in Kentucky. This jam session broke out in a parking lot in Rosine, near where the Father of Bluegrass, Bill Monroe, is buried.

The People

The state of Kentucky is growing and changing. In 1960, the state population was about three million. By 2010, it had increased to well over four million. Although that may seem like a lot of people, Kentucky's population is still not very large when compared to that of other states. Half of the fifty US states have more people than Kentucky.

The 2010 US census showed that about 88 percent of the state's people were white, or Caucasian. African Americans made up approximately 8 percent of the population, while Asian Americans represented around 1 percent. Just over 3 percent of residents identify themselves as Hispanic. There are few Native Americans living in the state, less than 0.2 percent of total residents.

The white people living in the state hail from many different backgrounds. Some are the descendants of the early pioneers, mostly of British ancestry, who settled in Kentucky when it was a remote and rugged frontier. Many other Kentuckians are descended from people who came in later years from other parts of the United States or abroad, seeking to build a new life.

When people are born in Kentucky, they tend to stay. In all, about seven out of ten residents of Kentucky today were born in the state. Only about 3 percent of Kentucky

Who Kentuckians Are

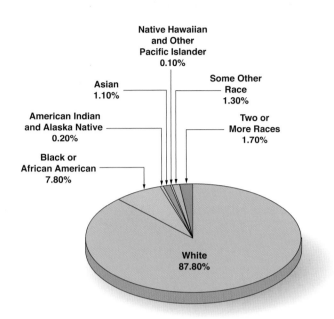

Native Hawaiian and Other Pacific Islander 0.10%

Some Other Race 1.30%

Asian 1.10%

American Indian and Alaska Native 0.20%

Two or More Races 1.70%

Black or African American 7.80%

White 87.80%

Total Population 4,339,367

Hispanic or Latino (of any race):
• 132,836 people (3.1%)

Note: The pie chart shows the racial breakdown of the state's population based on the categories used by the US Bureau of the Census. The Census Bureau reports information for Hispanics or Latinos separately, since they may be of any race. Percentages in the pie chart may not add to 100 because of rounding.

Source: US Bureau of the Census, 2010 Census

residents were born in a foreign country. This is much less than the US as a whole, where nearly 13 percent of the total population was born in another country.

One in five Kentuckians describes their background as simply "American," but many do identify with a particular ethnic group. About 17 percent of Kentucky's people describe their background as English, Scottish, Scots-Irish, or Welsh. Another 16 percent call themselves German, and 14 percent call themselves Irish. A number of others identify themselves as Italian, French, or Dutch.

African Americans

More than 330,000 African Americans live in Kentucky. African Americans first came to Kentucky as slaves and suffered hardships similar to other slaves in the South. While many residents opposed slavery during the 1800s, Kentucky did not end slavery on its own. Slavery was not abolished in the state until the Thirteenth Amendment to the US Constitution came into effect, months after the end of the Civil War.

Anti-black sentiment remained strong in parts of Kentucky after the war ended,

In Their Own Words

"To be born in Kentucky is a heritage; to brag about it is a habit; to appreciate it is a virtue."
—Irvin Cobb, author

African Americans comprise the largest minority group in Kentucky.

and many blacks had trouble finding jobs and raising themselves out of poverty. This discrimination continued into the 1900s, even as African Americans helped to build and fill the state's bustling cities. Many black citizens worked in the coal mines and factories. Conditions started to improve in the 1950s and 1960s as people throughout the state pushed for equal rights for Kentucky's black population.

Unfortunately, racial tensions still exist today, and many African Americans in Kentucky lag behind in income and education. Twice as many black students as white students drop out of school in grades seven to twelve. The average income of African Americans in Kentucky is about two-thirds that of whites. However, the income of African Americans has been rising over the years, and more and more of Kentucky's African Americans are able to live successful and prosperous lives. African Americans own more than ten thousand businesses in the state and are an important part of the state's workforce. Many take part in state and local government.

Hispanic Population

Hispanics, or Latinos, make up about 3 percent of the people in Kentucky. This population group has been growing rapidly in recent years. In 1990, there were only about 20,000

★ 10 ★ KEY PEOPLE ★ ★

Muhammad Ali

Johnny Depp

Jennifer Lawrence

1. Sophia Alcorn

Born in 1883 and a native of Stanford, Sophia Alcorn specialized in teaching disabled children. Alcorn developed the Tadoma Method to teach deaf and blind children to speak through the sense of touch. Her technique is still used today.

2. Muhammad Ali

Born Cassius Clay in 1942, in Louisville, boxing heavyweight champion Muhammad Ali faced racial discrimination growing up. He took his new name after converting to Islam in 1964. Ali won Olympic gold in 1960 and won the world heavyweight boxing championship three times.

3. Daniel Boone

Daniel Boone grew up with a love of the outdoors. In 1775, he blazed a trail through the Appalachians into what is now Kentucky, opening a way for settlers and becoming a hero of the American frontier.

4. Johnny Depp

Born in Owensboro in 1963, Johnny Depp starred in the television series *21 Jump Street* as well as many movies. He is best known for playing Captain Jack Sparrow in the *Pirates of the Caribbean* film series.

5. Jennifer Lawrence

Jennifer Lawrence was born in Louisville in 1990. She began acting at the age of fourteen and has starred in many films, including *X-Men: First Class* and *The Hunger Games*. Lawrence won an Academy Award for Best Actress in *Silver Linings Playbook* in 2013.

KENTUCKY

6. Loretta Lynn

Born in 1932 in rural Kentucky, Loretta Lynn grew up poor and married at fifteen. She moved to Nashville in 1960 to launch a singing career. The "Coal Miner's Daughter" was inducted into the Country Music Hall of Fame in 1988.

7. Suzan-Lori Parks

Playwright, novelist, and screenwriter Suzan-Lori Parks was born in Fort Knox in 1963. Encouraged by author James Baldwin to become a playwright, Parks became, in 2002, the first female African-American writer to win the Pulitzer Prize for Drama.

8. D'Angelo Russell

Born in Louisville, D'Angelo Russell was selected second overall by the Los Angeles Lakers in the 2015 National Basketball Association Draft. He played at Ohio State University, where he was an All-American.

9. Diane Sawyer

Born in Glasgow, Kentucky, in 1945, Diane Sawyer began her career at a TV station in Louisville. She became the first female correspondent for CBS's *60 Minutes* and an award-winning host for regular news programs on CBS and later ABC.

10. Whitney Young Jr.

Born in Lincoln Ridge in 1921, Whitney Young Jr. spent his life promoting education, jobs, and equal opportunity for African Americans. He advised several US presidents and received the Presidential Medal of Freedom in 1969.

Loretta Lynn

Suzan-Lori Parks

Diane Sawyer

Hispanic Americans in the state; that number rose to more than 130,000 in 2010. New immigrants from Mexico and countries in Central and South America come to Kentucky looking for better opportunities for themselves and their families.

Like other minorities, Hispanic Americans may often have to struggle, but many have found work on farms, in factories, and in other businesses. Some have established restaurants and stores that offer food and products from their homelands. Many of Kentucky's Hispanic residents take an active part in community and government activities.

Asian Americans

Asian Americans make up a fairly small population group in Kentucky. This group has been increasing as more and more immigrants arrive in the United States from the largest continent, Asia. There were more than twice as many Kentuckians of Asian descent in 2010 as there had been twenty years earlier. Like other minorities, Asian Americans make an important contribution to the life and culture of the state.

Native Americans

Native Americans are only a tiny minority of Kentucky's population today. Even when the earliest white pioneers settled in the region that is now Kentucky, not many Native Americans lived there. Those who did, or who came at different times to hunt, found their way of life disrupted by the arrival of Europeans. Many died from diseases that the Europeans carried. Others either moved away by choice or were forced to move by settlers or the US government.

Kentucky has no Native American reservations. The state's Native American population has, however, increased a bit in recent years. There are about ten thousand Native Americans living in Kentucky today. Festivals and other gatherings held across the state help keep the state's Native American heritage alive and give residents and visitors a chance to learn more about Native American history and culture.

Mainly Christian

Throughout its history under white settlers, Kentucky has been predominantly Christian and mostly Protestant. Baptists, Methodists, Presbyterians, and Roman Catholics had established themselves by the time Kentucky became a state. Evangelical Protestantism is predominant today, but people also practice their Roman Catholic, Jewish, and Muslim faiths. While most Kentuckians are religious, about 46 percent of Kentucky's people identify themselves as not belonging to any formal religious organization.

The Shakers Arrive

Among the settlers of English descent who came to Kentucky in the 1800s were the Shakers. This Christian movement practiced separation from the rest of the world. The name Shaker was actually given to this religious group as a **derisive** term by people outside the faith who had watched the Shakers whirl and tremble to "shake" off sins and evil during their worship.

The movement spread throughout New England and later into Kentucky, Ohio, and Indiana. Shakers became admired around the world for their simply designed furniture and fine crafts. The Shakers did not believe in marriage or having children, relying on getting converts to expand their religion. Today, a community with a few Shakers exists in Maine, but Shaker settlements in Kentucky (and most other states) have vanished. Visitors can tour the restored Shaker Village of Pleasant Hill, near Harrodsburg, to learn about Shaker culture and history.

Maysville is among the many beautiful small cities in Kentucky.

Where Kentuckians Live

Kentucky started out as a rugged frontier region and, until the 1960s, most Kentuckians lived in rural areas. Today, however, three out of five people live in urban areas. Most of these people live in northern Kentucky and the cities of Louisville and Lexington. This area, where most of the jobs are, is known as the Golden Triangle.

As of the 2010 census, Louisville, the state's biggest city, had a population of almost six hundred thousand. Close to three hundred thousand people lived in Lexington, Kentucky's second-largest city. Other major cities in the state include Bowling Green, Owensboro, Covington, Hopkinsville, Richmond,

Florence, and Georgetown, along with Frankfort, the capital, but only Lexington and Louisville have populations of more than sixty thousand. While the Golden Triangle region has grown steadily in recent years, the population has declined in many other parts of the state.

Downtown Louisville has many historic buildings, some of which are more than 150 years old. The historic district known as Old Louisville is one of the largest districts of its kind in the United States. Modern skyscrapers can also be found in the city, however. The new Waterfront Park along the Ohio River provides plenty of open space for Kentuckians to enjoy. Every spring, the Kentucky Derby and its related events attract hundreds of thousands of visitors to the city.

The other towns and cities in Kentucky have their own history, traditions, and festivals. Some towns are on the outskirts of cities and have malls, large office buildings, and other urban features. Others lie farther into the countryside. A number of towns were founded originally to provide homes for miners or loggers and their families. Many of those towns suffered when mines or logging operations shut down and workers lost their jobs, forcing families to move away. Today, these towns may have only a handful of people and a few dilapidated buildings, while other towns and small cities have grown and prospered.

Poverty in Appalachia

Life in the Appalachian Mountains of Kentucky can be very hard. Many families live in remote locations, far from towns and even from other families. They may have to travel a great distance to reach stores and schools. Jobs are in short supply, and those who do have jobs often work in the mines, which can be dangerous and hazardous to their health. However, many people in Appalachia come from families that have lived in the region for generations. They have adapted to the challenging conditions and appreciate living in a place of great beauty.

Fun in Kentucky

Kentuckians have many ways to enjoy themselves. For one thing, they know how to cheer on their favorite sports teams. While the state does not have any major-league professional teams, Kentuckians are proud of their Triple-A Minor League Baseball team, the Louisville Bats.

As for college sports, Kentucky is a national powerhouse. The University of Kentucky (UK) fields top football and basketball teams. In 2012, UK won the National Collegiate Athletic Association (NCAA) Men's Division I Basketball Championship for the eighth time. The sports rivalry between the UK Wildcats and the University of Louisville Cardinals, another college power, is famous. Other well-known teams include the men's and women's basketball teams at Western Kentucky University.

Outdoor Beauty

Kentuckians love the outdoors. Scattered around the state are more than thirty state parks and forests, along with beautiful places such as Mammoth Cave National Park, Land Between the Lakes National Recreation Area, and Daniel Boone National Forest. Hiking, camping, boating, and fishing are popular pastimes for residents and for visitors from out of state. Residents and visitors alike come to Louisville to enjoy the Kentucky State Fair, held each August. Many other festivals, fairs, and special events are held throughout the year in different parts of the state.

The Cumberland Falls is a popular destination for rafters.

Kentucky also has dozens of museums and historical sites, ranging from the International Bluegrass Music Museum, in Owensboro, to Abraham Lincoln's birthplace, near Hodgenville, and the Civil War battlefields of Richmond and Perryville. Many of Kentucky's popular attractions are in Louisville, including the Louisville Science Center, the recently renovated Speed Art Museum, the Kentucky Derby Museum, and the Louisville Slugger Museum and Factory, with exhibits on the history of the famous Louisville Slugger baseball bats.

The Kentucky Derby is probably the state's most popular event. This world-famous horse race for three-year-old Thoroughbreds, the first leg of the **Triple Crown**, has been held in Louisville every May since 1875. It is a stirring moment when the horses parade to the gate and the band plays the state's official song, "My Old Kentucky Home." Each year, in the last weeks before the race, Louisville hosts the Kentucky Derby Festival, which includes concerts, parades, races, and a spectacular fireworks display, said to be one of the biggest in the world.

Festival of the Horse

1. Apple Blossom Festival

This event, held in Elkhorn City every May since 1976, celebrates springtime in the mountains. It includes a parade, crafts, music, carnival rides, a car show, and different kinds of local food, as well as a train ride through town.

2. Eagle Watch Weekends

On weekends in January and February, state parks around Kentucky, including Kentucky Dam Village State Resort Park in the southwest, host this event. Visitors take the opportunity to view bald eagles in their natural habitat.

3. Festival of the Horse

Georgetown hosts this celebration each fall. Parades, carnival rides, sports competitions, and live entertainment, along with a horse show, celebrate the horse's importance in Kentucky history and culture. In 2015, the festival marked its thirty-fifth year.

4. Great American Brass Band Festival

Held in Danville each June since 1990, the Great American Brass Band Festival features the sounds of brass music and the smells of delicious foods wafting through the air. The event is dedicated to preserving brass band music.

5. Highland Games in Glasgow

Scottish traditions and culture are honored each June at the Glasgow Highland Games. The festival began in 1986 to celebrate the town's Celtic roots. The Barren County community takes its name from Glasgow, Scotland.

Great American Brass Band Festival

KENTUCKY ★ ★ ★ ★

6. Kentucky Derby Festival

For two weeks in the spring, right before the Kentucky Derby, Louisville puts on a splashy festival with many events for kids, including fireworks, steamboat and balloon races, and concerts. Hundreds of thousands join in the celebration.

7. Kentucky State Fair

This August event is held at the Louisville State Fairgrounds. Each year, some six hundred thousand people enjoy exhibits featuring agricultural and livestock competitions, craft contests, and musical performances, as well as rides, games, and food.

8. MainStrasse Village Oktoberfest

More than one hundred thousand people visit the MainStrasse Village in Covington each October for this festival of food, music, and arts and crafts celebrating the area's German heritage. Its location just across the Ohio River from Cincinnati adds to the attendance.

9. Trail of Tears Powwow

Hopkinsville, Kentucky, was one of the places where Native American Cherokees stopped during their forced journey to Oklahoma, known as the Trail of Tears. Each September, the area celebrates Native American history and culture.

10. World Chicken Festival

This festival is held at the end of September in downtown London, in Laurel County, home of the world's first Kentucky Fried Chicken restaurant. This event celebrates that heritage with eating contests, sports competitions, and parades.

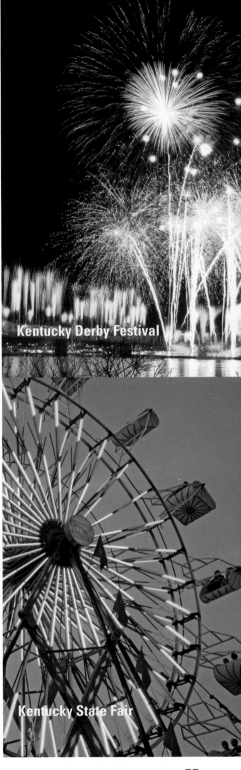

Kentucky Derby Festival

Kentucky State Fair

Portraits of past governors line
the Kentucky Hall of Governors
in the Thomas D. Clark Center for
Kentucky History in the capital
city of Frankfort.

How the Government Works

Like other states, Kentucky's government serves its people on many levels. Cities and towns form the lowest level. They are usually run by a mayor or by a city or town manager, along with some form of council to make local laws. It is the responsibility of these local government leaders, and their employees, to make sure their city or town runs well and provides needed services, from street cleaning and waste removal to police and fire protection. The most important duty for local leaders is to listen to residents or community groups who have questions about their government or the laws.

Counties represent the next-highest level of government. All of the state's cities and towns are located within one of Kentucky's 120 counties. County governments have responsibilities in such areas as courts and law enforcement. They are generally run by a governing body called the fiscal court, which includes a county judge and commissioners. County governments are especially important in sparsely populated areas, where many people live outside of towns and cities. These people depend more on county governments for services.

Kentucky's two largest cities are Louisville and Lexington. The governments of both cities have merged with the governments of the counties in which they are located, so for

The residence for the governor was completed in 1914. It is on the capitol grounds and is open for tours.

these two areas, the city and county governments are combined. However, towns within these counties still have separate local governments.

The highest level of Kentucky's government is the state. State government is responsible for matters that affect Kentucky as a whole. Transportation, the environment, business and economic growth, public health and safety—these are among many areas where the state has a major role to play. Education is also an important responsibility for the state. The state board of education makes sure that schools in each district maintain standards required by the state. The state also runs eight public universities. The largest is the University of Kentucky.

The basic rules for governing the state are outlined in Kentucky's current constitution, which has been in effect since 1891. It replaced three earlier constitutions. Over the years, the state constitution has been changed, or amended, forty times.

Branches of Government

Like the federal and other state governments, Kentucky's government is made up of three branches: executive, legislative, and judicial. Each branch has its own responsibilities.

Executive

The governor runs the state government, puts together the state budget, and approves or rejects (vetoes) measures passed by lawmakers. The governor is elected to a four-year term and cannot serve more than two terms in a row. The lieutenant governor, who is elected with the governor, takes over if the governor is unable to perform his or her duties. Certain other state officials, such as the attorney general, treasurer, and secretary of state, are also elected for four-year terms. Many other officials are appointed by the governor.

Legislative

Kentucky's law-making body, or state legislature, is known as the Kentucky General Assembly. It is divided into two parts, or chambers—the senate and the house of representatives. The senate has thirty-eight members who serve four-year terms. Every two years, half of the senate positions come up for election. The house has one hundred members, elected for two-year terms. There is no limit on the number of terms that members of the legislature can serve.

The state legislature meets in the capitol, which was opened in 1910.

Judicial

The judicial branch, called the Kentucky Court of Justice, consists of four levels of state courts: district courts, circuit courts, the court of **appeals**, and the supreme court. District courts hear a limited range of cases, including those concerned with traffic violations, small crimes called misdemeanors, and civil disputes involving less than $5,000.

Circuit courts decide more serious cases. They also hear certain appeals from district courts. The court of appeals hears appeals from lower courts. It has fourteen justices who serve on rotating panels of three that travel around the state to hear cases. The supreme court is Kentucky's highest court and hears certain appeals, including

The Paris Opera House inspired this magnificent marble staircase inside the capitol.

any appeal of a death penalty case or a sentence of twenty or more years in prison. There are seven supreme court justices, each elected for an eight-year term. The supreme court can overturn a state law if it is found to violate the state constitution.

Based in Frankfort

The general assembly and the supreme court meet in the state capitol, in Frankfort. This is also where the governor's office is located. Kentuckians often boast that their capitol is among the most beautiful buildings of its kind in the United States. It was built in the French style known as Beaux Arts. The governor's mansion (official residence) is also located in Frankfort.

US Congress

Kentucky also sends representatives to the US Congress in Washington, DC. Like voters from all states, Kentucky voters elect two people to serve six-year terms in the US Senate. Kentuckians also elect six members to the US House of Representatives, where they serve two-year terms. This number of representatives is based on the state's population from the latest census, in 2010. These federal legislators represent Kentucky's interests and concerns when it comes to governing the nation.

Silly Law

A state law in Kentucky requires every resident to bathe at least once each year.

How a Bill Becomes a Law

A state law starts out as a bill. The idea for a bill can come from state legislators or from ordinary citizens. However, only representatives or senators can formally introduce a bill into the legislature.

After the bill is introduced in the house or senate, it is given a number and assigned to a committee for consideration. The committee may also decide to hold a public hearing, where citizens can present their opinions about the bill. If committee members support passing the bill, it has a first reading by the whole house or senate and will move on for a second reading.

After the second reading, it is sent to the Rules Committee. If the Rules Committee approves the measure, it is again presented to the whole house or senate. Members debate and may agree to amend—or change—the bill. If a version of the bill is approved by a majority of those present, and by two-fifths of the total membership, it passes to the other house.

Once in the other house, the proposed bill moves through the same process. If the version of the bill passed in one house differs from the version passed in the other, it may be sent to a joint conference committee to resolve the differences. Both houses must then approve the final version. Once both houses pass the bill, it is read again and prepared for the governor. The governor may approve or reject the bill. If the governor simply fails to act on the bill for ten days, it is considered approved. If the governor rejects the bill, it can still be passed if a majority of the members of both houses votes to approve it.

People Taking Part

Kentuckians may get involved in politics and government in different ways. A few run for election to political office. Others participate in political campaigns or contribute money to candidates they support. Many people attend and speak at public hearings and meetings, or contact elected officials to support or oppose a piece of legislation. Finally, many adults participate in politics by voting on Election Day.

If you want to get more involved, the first step is to learn more about issues and problems that interest you. Follow the news through radio, TV, print or online newspapers, or the websites of other news organizations. If you want to support a particular cause or position, send an e-mail or a letter to your state senator or representative.

POLITICAL FIGURES
FROM KENTUCKY

Henry Clay: US Senator, 1831–1842 and 1849–1852.

Born in Virginia in 1777, Henry Clay moved to Kentucky and served as a US congressman before being elected to the Senate. Clay was known as the Great Compromiser for working out agreements related to slavery that delayed the Civil War. Among those were the Missouri Compromise of 1820 and the Compromise of 1850. He also served as secretary of state under President John Quincy Adams.

Martha Layne Collins: Governor, 1983–1987

Born in Shelby County in 1936, Martha Layne Collins taught in public schools before entering politics. She was elected lieutenant governor of Kentucky in 1979, and in 1983, she was elected as Kentucky's first and only female governor. She also chaired the 1984 Democratic National Convention.

Mitch McConnell: US Senator, 1985–

Senator Mitch McConnell, who grew up in Louisville, has represented Kentucky in the US Senate since 1985. That is longer than any other senator from the state. McConnell, who is a Republican, became leader of his party in the Senate in 2007, and became Senate majority leader in 2015.

KENTUCKY ★ ★ ★
YOU CAN MAKE A DIFFERENCE

Contacting Lawmakers

To find contact information for Kentucky's state legislators, go to:

www.lrc.ky.gov/kidspages/find%20legislators.htm

Click on the county that you live in and you will see links to your senators and representatives. Click on their link to get more information about them and the area they represent. An adult such as a parent, teacher, or librarian can also help you.

To contact your US representatives, go to:

www.govtrack.us/congress/members/KY

Click on their names to find out contact information. There is a link below each congressperson's photo to a map of the district they represent. Click on that link if you are unsure of the district in which you live.

Legacy in Law for Anna

After a Kentucky newborn was diagnosed with a deadly genetic disease, her parents worked with the state legislature to pass "Anna's Law." The new law made it easier for families to find out if their babies have the disease and to provide medical treatment in time to help the children.

Anna Taylor was born on April 28, 2013. She passed all of her health tests and was a happy, healthy baby until she was four months old. When she suddenly became very sick, doctors found that Anna had Krabbe disease, a very rare condition that is almost always found in babies. It affects the nervous system and usually causes death by the age of two.

Doctors have had some success in treating Krabbe disease, but it happened only when babies were tested and treated before they showed any symptoms. While some states already required testing for Krabbe disease for all newborns, Kentucky at that time did not. Even though Anna could not be cured, Anna's parents worked with Kentucky state senator Alice Kerr to revise Kentucky's laws so that the test for Krabbe disease would be included for all Kentucky babies in the future. "Anna's Law" was signed by the governor in March 2015, shortly before Anna passed away.

Manufacturing cars has become an
increasingly important business in

Making a Living

The state of Kentucky has close to two million workers. Some of them work as farmers or miners, like so many Kentuckians in the past. Many others are employed in factories, making products that people buy and use, or in construction, building homes and highways.

Kentucky's economy is changing, however. Today, most people in Kentucky work in what are called service jobs, providing services to people rather than building or manufacturing things. Service jobs include working in stores, restaurants, hospitals, schools, or offices. Some involve working for local or state government. Tourism provides many service jobs, and banking, finance, and insurance are also important. Humana, one of the nation's biggest health insurance companies, has its headquarters in Louisville. It is by far the biggest publicly owned company in the state.

Fertile Land

Kentucky's fertile soil has been a source of livelihood for centuries. The soil is what drew pioneers to the area in the early years of white settlement, and Kentucky was at first mainly a farming state. Even today, Kentucky has more than eighty thousand farms. About nine out of ten are family farms, and more than half of all Kentucky's farms are smaller than 100 acres (40 ha).

Farmers still grow a lot of tobacco, which is an important crop in the state.

While Kentucky grows many crops, one that has a very long history in the state is tobacco. Historians say that Native Americans living in the area thousands of years ago smoked tobacco that grew wild there. Early white settlers grew tobacco to sell, sending it to factories in Louisville, where it was made into cigars, snuff, and chewing and pipe tobacco. Once cigarettes became popular in the early twentieth century, tobacco became Kentucky's most important crop.

The demand for tobacco has fallen in the US over the past few decades as people learned about the serious health risks of smoking and breathing secondhand smoke. There still are tobacco farms and factories across the state, and tobacco is still a leading product and major export in Kentucky. However, the future for tobacco—and people who make a living from it—is uncertain. Some farmers who once grew tobacco have turned to growing other crops.

In fact, corn, soybeans, and hay already make more money than tobacco for Kentucky's farmers. Wheat and fruits and vegetables are other major farm crops. Kentucky's most important farm product of all is breeding and selling chickens. Beef cattle also provide a major source of income for Kentucky farmers.

Horses Are Big Business

Kentucky is especially well known for its Thoroughbred horses. In the Bluegrass region, white fences surround huge pastures where horses graze on the lush grass. Horses bred in Kentucky are sold to customers within the state, around the country, and around the world. Most of the horses are used for racing, although some perform in show jumping and other competitions. In 2010, the Thoroughbred breeding industry provided jobs for almost twenty thousand Kentuckians.

Wealth from Coal

Early settlers discovered that Kentucky's mountains were rich in coal deposits, and coal mining quickly became a key industry in the nineteenth century. Coal was needed to fuel steamboats and trains, to heat buildings, and to power machinery in factories. While mining is still important to Kentucky's economy, jobs in the industry started declining in the 1980s. Even so, as of 2010, Kentucky was still the country's third-biggest coal-producing state, after Wyoming and West Virginia. The two main coalfields can be found in the eastern and western sections of the state.

Kentucky remains one of the largest coal-producing states.

★ 10 KEY★INDUSTRIES

Cars and Trucks

Cattle

1. Biotechnology and Life Sciences

Biotechnology and life science companies work with living organisms to make valuable products. More than ninety-three thousand people work at Kentucky's biotechnology companies, which include major research centers such as the University of Kentucky and the University of Louisville.

2. Cars and Trucks

Auto manufacturing is a top Kentucky industry, supporting more than sixty-five thousand jobs. Toyota, Ford, and General Motors operate major assembly plants. In recent years, Kentucky has ranked third among the states in production of cars and trucks.

3. Cattle

Kentucky is the eighth-largest beef cow producing state in the United States and the largest east of the Mississippi River. Kentucky has more than one million head of cattle, and livestock products account for about half of Kentucky's farm income.

4. Chemicals

In 2015, the chemical industry ranked third among all state industries, accounting for nearly twenty thousand jobs. Paints, cleaning chemicals, and medical drugs are some of the products produced in the state.

5. Coal

Although Kentucky's coal production has declined recently, the state still produced more than 80 million tons (71 million metric tons) in 2013, about 8 percent of the total US production. Kentucky remains the third-biggest coal producer.

6. Corn

Corn is Kentucky's biggest crop today. Much of Kentucky's corn is used to feed livestock raised on farms. Some of it is made into bourbon, a kind of whiskey. About 95 percent of the world's bourbon is made in Kentucky.

7. Government

Kentucky's government actually ranks as the state's second-largest industry in terms of the number of employees. In 2015, more than 325,000 people worked at some level for the state. The government says its mission is to "attract … and retain a talented, diverse workforce."

8. Horses

Horses are big business in Kentucky. Horses and related businesses account for $3 billion in annual economic impact and create almost forty-one thousand jobs, according a 2013 University of Kentucky economic analysis. The equine industry generates about $134 million in tax revenue.

9. Tourism

Kentucky's mountains, forests, lakes, and caves attract visitors. Tourism provides many jobs, a big help to the state in difficult economic times. It generated more than $13 billion in economic impact in 2014.

10. Transportation

Kentucky is a center of transportation and **logistics** services. Highways, railroads, river ports, and airports help businesses ship goods worldwide Shipping companies UPS and DHL operate major facilities in the state

Corn

Horses

Recipe for Kentucky Jam Cake

This traditional three-layer Kentucky cake is made with seedless blackberry jam and a variety of spices, and it is usually topped with caramel or cream cheese frosting

What You Need

8 ounces (227 grams) butter, softened

2 cups (473 milliliters) sugar

5 eggs

3 cups (710 mL) flour

1 teaspoon (5 mL) baking soda

½ teaspoon (2.5 mL) salt

½ teaspoon (2.5 mL) ground cloves

1 teaspoon (5 mL) ground allspice

1 teaspoon (5 mL) ground cinnamon

½ teaspoon (2.5 mL) ground nutmeg

1 cup (237 mL) buttermilk

1 cup (237 mL) seedless blackberry jam

1 cup (237 mL) chopped pecans

1 cup (237 mL) chopped raisins or dates

Frosting

What To Do

- Mix butter and sugar until creamy.

- Add eggs and beat well, one at a time.

- Combine flour, baking soda, salt, and spices in a separate bowl.

- Add to the first mixture a little at a time, alternating with buttermilk and beating well after each addition.

- Blend in the jam, chopped pecans, and raisins or dates.

- Pour into three greased and floured 8- to 9-inch (20–23 cm) round cake pans.

- Bake at 325°F (163°C) for 35 to 40 minutes, or until the center is cooked.

- Cool in pans on racks for 15 minutes.

- Frost with caramel frosting or cream cheese frosting.

Safety and Concern About the Environment

Although underground coal mining in the United States is much safer than it once was, it still is a dangerous job. Miners face cave-ins and explosions, as well as hazards from unseen gases such as methane and carbon monoxide. The dust and fumes in the mines are also hazardous to health. The last major coal mine disaster in Kentucky happened in 2006, in Middlesboro, when five miners were killed in an explosion.

Meanwhile, a method called surface mining has raised serious environmental concerns, especially since the 1960s, when "mountaintop removal" became common. In this type of mining, workers use explosives to blast away rock and soil at the tops of mountains or hills to expose seams of coal that may lie well beneath the surface. The mining industry argues that this method is safer and more efficient than underground mining, but others believe that mining in this way hurts the environment and damages the land for future generations.

In 1998, a coal-mining company wanted to start surface mining on Black Mountain, Kentucky's highest mountain. Seventh-grade students at Wallins Creek, an elementary school near the mountain, organized a class project to try to prevent this from happening. They raised money for a field trip and spent two days studying plants and animals that live on the mountain. They also talked to other people who lived nearby and visited other strip-mining sites.

Using the information they had gathered, the students spoke to adult voters about why they thought the strip mining should not be allowed. They also sent e-mails and letters to government officials. Their grassroots campaign helped draw attention to the issue, and in the end, huge areas of the mountain were saved from surface mining.

Federal law now requires that in most cases the land must be restored to its original shape and use. However, the process still disrupts the environment and can lead to problems such as water pollution and flooding. Despite these problems, coal remains an important source of energy today, and many Kentuckians still depend on coal mining for their livelihood.

Making Things

For a long time, farming and mining were the main industries of Kentucky. By the 1930s, however, manufacturing became more important. After 1945, there was a huge increase in factory jobs. New industries came to Kentucky because of its large supply of coal and the low cost of electricity. Over the years, manufacturing became a major source of income.

Manufacturing still plays a key role in Kentucky's economy, even though some jobs have been lost due to problems in the US economy and an increase in cheaper goods coming from other countries. Today, Kentucky boasts the eighth-highest share of employment in manufacturing among the states, 3.6 percentage points higher than the national average.

Nearly 13 percent of the workers in Kentucky today have manufacturing jobs. Motor vehicles have become one of the state's most important products. Almost 10 percent of all cars and trucks made in the United States come from factories in Kentucky. The biggest Toyota manufacturing plant in the world is located in Georgetown.

Kentucky factories also manufacture appliances, aircraft parts, chemicals, electrical equipment, food products, textiles, metal products, and bourbon, a kind of whiskey for which the state is famous. These manufacturing jobs help bring much-needed tax revenue to the state and also employ many Kentuckians.

Though most Kentucky products come from factories, some items are still handmade. During the state's early history, Kentuckians had to make for themselves many of the things that they used every day. Families built their own furniture, including beds, tables,

In Their Own Words

"Recent changes in the energy economy have had a profound impact on Appalachian families and communities that have been sustained by the coal industry for generations."
—US secretary of labor Thomas E. Perez

and rocking chairs. Women wove rugs and sewed the quilts their families used. Some Kentuckians whittled toys and fishing rods, while others made clay pots, and folk artists produced paintings and sculptures. Many Kentucky craftspeople make their living today by selling the beautiful objects they create.

Tourism

Tourism is an important and growing industry in Kentucky. The state attracts visitors from all over the United States and many parts of the world. Many come to attend business conventions or special events such as the Kentucky Derby. Others visit to enjoy the state's fantastic natural wonders, including Cumberland Falls, Red River Gorge, Mammoth Cave, and the state's many parks and forests.

The practice of strip mining has harmed the environment in Kentucky.

The jobs created by tourism help many Kentuckians make a living. Many state residents work in the hotels, restaurants, shops, and attractions that tourists visit. In 2010, tourism employed about 170,000 Kentuckians, contributed about $11 billion to the state economy and provided more than $1 billion in taxes to state and local governments.

Finding a Balance

Humans have lived off Kentucky's land for thousands of years. In recent centuries, Kentucky's residents have radically changed the land to meet their needs. Farmers have cleared woodlands and loggers have cut down forests. Cities and towns have replaced woods and fields. Coal mining has stripped away land, sometimes without restoring it adequately. Chemical plants and other factories have sometimes released **toxic** waste into the land and water.

Today's world is very different from the one settlers encountered when they traveled on the Wilderness Road to come to Kentucky and build farms and villages. Kentuckians rely on the industries of today to support themselves and their families, and more needs to be done to provide better opportunities to people who are struggling. In the future, the people will have to strike a balance between human needs and the need to preserve the environment so that Kentucky can remain beautiful and safe while providing a livelihood for workers and their families.

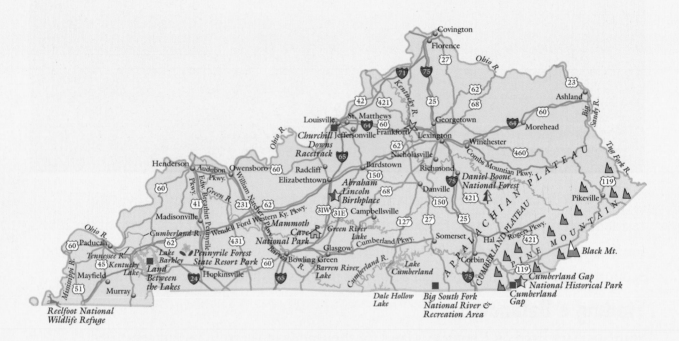

Covington
Florence
27
Ohio R.
71 75
62
Kentucky R.
23
25
42 421
68
Ashland
60
Louisville St. Matthews
64
60
Georgetown
64 Morehead
Churchill Jeffersonville Frankfort Lexington
Big Sandy R.
Downs
Racetrack
65
62
Winchester
460
Combs Mountain Pkwy.
Tug Fork R.
Henderson
Bardstown
Nicholasville
Audubon Owensboro
60
Radcliff
150
Richmond
Daniel Boone
Pkwy.
119
60
Elizabethtown
68
Danville
National Forest
Pikeville
Green R.
Abraham
75
APPALACHIAN PLATEAU
41
Lincoln
150
Edw. Breathitt Pennyrile
William Natcher Pkwy.
Birthplace
421
Madisonville
231
62
31W 31E
Campbellsville
25
Wendell Ford Western Ky. Pkwy.
Mammoth
127
27
Rogers Pkwy.
Black Mt.
Cumberland R.
Cave
Green River
Ohio R.
62
National Park
Lake
Somerset
Hal
421
PINE MOUNTAIN
Paducah
431
Glasgow
Cumberland Pkwy.
CUMBERLAND PLATEAU
Tennessee R.
Lake
119
45 Kentucky
Barkley
Bowling Green
Corbin
Mayfield
Lake
Barren River
Cumberland Gap
Land
60
Lake
75
National Historical Park
51
Between
24
Hopkinsville
Lake
119
Cumberland
Murray
the Lakes
Cumberland
Gap
Reelfoot National
Dale Hollow
Big South Fork
Wildlife Refuge
Lake
National River &
Recreation Area

KENTUCKY ★ ★ ★
MAP SKILLS

1. **What Kentucky city lies farthest north in the state?**

2. **The Land Between the Lakes sits between what two Kentucky lakes?**

3. **The Cumberland Gap is located in what corner of Kentucky: northeast, northwest, southeast, or southwest?**

4. **What major interstate highway links the cities of Florence in north to Corbin in the south?**

5. **What famous racetrack is located near Louisville?**

6. **What is Kentucky's highest mountain?**

7. **What is Kentucky's state capital city?**

8. **What national park can be found southwest of Abraham Lincoln's birthplace?**

9. **Daniel Boone National Forest is located close to what plateau that stretches all the way across Kentucky?**

10. **What three rivers are located in the southwest corner of Kentucky?**

Churchill Downs Racetrack

1. Covington
2. Kentucky Lake and Lake Barkley
3. Southeast
4. Interstate 75
5. Churchill Downs Racetrack
6. Black Mt.
7. Frankfort
8. Mammoth Cave National Park
9. The Appalachian Plateau
10. The Ohio, Mississippi, and Tennessee Rivers.

Black Mountain

State Flag, Seal, and Song

The Kentucky General Assembly first adopted the state flag on March 26, 1918. The final version of the flag, designed by an art teacher in Frankfort named Jesse Cox, was adopted in 1928. The state flag consists of the state seal on a navy blue background.

The state seal, originally adopted in 1792, shows two men shaking hands. One is a frontiersman, dressed in buckskin, who represents Kentucky's country residents. The other is a statesman, dressed in a formal suit, who represents those living in Kentucky's cities. The state motto, "United We Stand, Divided We Fall," is printed in a circle around the two figures. The words were taken from "The Liberty Song," a popular song from the American Revolution. The outer border of the seal displays the words "Commonwealth of Kentucky" and a wreath of goldenrod, the state flower. The official colors of the seal are blue and gold.

Kentucky's state song is "My Old Kentucky Home, Good-Night!" It was adopted by the state legislature as the Kentucky state song in 1928, and the lyrics were later updated in 1986. It was written by Stephen Foster in 1853. To view the lyrics, visit:

www.uky.edu/KentuckyCulture/my-old-kentucky-home.html

Glossary

appeals In the legal system, requests to a higher court to change a decision that was already made in a lower court.

convergence Where two or more rivers, roads, or air currents meet.

council A group elected or chosen to discuss issues and make decisions.

derisive The feeling that people express when they criticize or laugh at someone or something in an insulting way.

ecological The relationship between living things and their environment.

jut Something extending outward, like a peninsula into an ocean.

logistics The business of planning events and transporting goods and services to customers.

plots In real estate, small pieces or areas of land.

prohibited Forbidden or not allowed.

stock market A marketplace where people can buy and sell ownership shares of companies.

Thoroughbred A pure breed of horse developed for speed and jumping ability in England by crossing Arabian stallions with European mares.

toxic Poisonous or dangerous, something that can harm your health.

Trail of Tears The route along which the United States government forced Native American tribes to move from their lands in the Deep South to areas west of the Mississippi River in the 1830s, during which thousands died from exposure and starvation.

Triple Crown In horse racing, the title awarded to a three-year-old Thoroughbred horse which wins the Kentucky Derby (in Kentucky), the Preakness Stakes (in Maryland), and the Belmont Stakes (in New York).

venomous Describing snakes or other creatures that can inject their venom, or poison, into another creature to paralyze or kill it.

More About Kentucky

BOOKS

Burton, K. Melissa, and James Asher. *Now That's Interesting: Kentucky's Capitol*. Kuttawa, KY: McClanahan Publishing, 2007.

Howell, Brian. *Kentucky Wildcats*. Inside College Basketball. Minneapolis, MN: SportsZone, 2012.

Ludwick, Cameron, and Blair Thomas Hess. *My Old Kentucky Road Trip: Historic Destinations and Natural Wonders*. Mount Pleasant, SC: Arcadia Publishing, 2015.

Santella, Andrew. *Daniel Boone and the Cumberland Gap*. Cornerstones of Freedom. Danbury, CT: Children's Press, 2007.

WEBSITES

Kentucky State Parks

parks.ky.gov

Official Kentucky State Web Site

www.kentucky.gov

Kentucky Legislature Kids' Pages

www.lrc.ky.gov/kidspages/kids.htm

ABOUT THE AUTHORS

Ann Graham Gaines is a freelance writer and photo researcher who lives near Gonzales, Texas. Kentucky is one of her favorite places to visit.

William McGeveran is a freelance editor and writer who formerly was the editorial director at World Almanac Books. He is a grandfather who lives in the New York City area.

Gerry Boehme was born in New York City, graduated from the Newhouse School at Syracuse University and now lives on Long Island with his wife and two children.

Index

Page numbers in **boldface** are illustrations. Entries in **boldface** are glossary terms.

Index

DISCARD

J 976.9 GAINES

Gaines, Ann.
Kentucky

R4002925052

Atlanta-Fulton Public Library